PREFACE

The purpose of this edition is to make available one of the most attractive of Monteverdi's *concertato* sacred compositions in a form which presents an authentic text and is at the same time suitable for performance. To achieve this, some additions and alterations have been necessary; these are all clearly distinguishable from the original, as enumerated at the end of this Preface.

Monteverdi published his *Selva Morale* as late as 1641, although the collection contains music dating back to at least 1611. The close relationship between the musical material of *Beatus Vir* and that of the *concertato* madrigal *Chiome d'oro* (from the seventh book of madrigals, 1619) has often been pointed out.[1] Redlich suggests that *Beatus Vir* dates from before 1610, but this is very doubtful. The work is not only organized on a broader scale than Monteverdi's earlier church music (compare the quasi-mosaic structures of the psalm and Magnificat settings in the Vespers of 1610), but also the ritornello and recurrent bass patterns of *Chiome d'oro* have undergone a major expansion. It is in fact a parody psalm, analogous to the parody Mass. Furthermore, *Beatus Vir* shares many features in common with another work from the *Selva Morale*, the *Gloria concertata* which both Schrade and Arnold agree in dating from 1631. This evidence, together with the giant da capo form of the work, suggests a date some time about 1630.

Source

Selva morale et spirituale di Claudio Monteverde maestro di capella della Serenissima Republica di Venetia dedicata alla Sacra Cesarea Maestà della Imperatrice Eleonora Gonzaga con licenza de Superiori, & Priuilegio. In Venetia MDCXXXXI Appresso Bartolomeo Magni.

Ten part-books: *Soprano Primo, Soprano Secondo, Alto Primo, Alto e Basso Secondo, Tenore Primo, Tenore Secondo, Basso Primo, Violino Primo, Violino Secondo, Basso Continuo*. (The fourth of these is not needed for the present composition). Original full title (from *Tavola* at end of *Basso Continuo*); *Beatus Primo à 6 voci concertato con due violini & 3 viole da brazzo ouero 3 Tromboni quali anco si ponno lasciare.*

This edition has been transcribed from a microfilm of the copy in the Library of the Gesellschaft der Musikfreunde, Vienna. No other copy has been consulted, except the modern edition by G. Francesco Malipiero in *Tutte le opere di Claudio Monteverdi*, vol. 15 (1941). Malipiero reproduces the title page of the *Tenore Secondo* book as a frontispiece to this volume; this differs in design from that of the Vienna set, and is dated 1640, not 1641 (the dedication is dated 1 May 1641).

Instrumentation and performance

The trombone parts are of course not included in the original set of part-books. However, the full title of the piece says: 'with 3 viole da brazzo or 3 trombones, which may however be omitted'. These instruments were intended to double the three lowest voice parts, a common enough practice of the time. The Editor prefers trombones, since they have proved their effectiveness in performances with which he has been associated. Doubtless two violas and a cello would be more suitable for a very small scale performance, or even, as Monteverdi suggests, the omission of all doubling whatsoever. Sections where fewer than the full number of six voices are singing may of course be taken by soloists, preferably from the choir. In this case trombone doubling should be omitted.

The two obbligato violins can be solo or ripieno. Solo instruments are quite sufficient against a choir of 30 strong, about the number Monteverdi had at his disposal at St. Mark's, Venice. The continuo sounds best on an organ with one or two cellos doubling the bass line for added definition. Registration should consist of bright and transparent flue stops only, throwing the voices and instruments into relief rather than attempting to compete with them. Pedals, says Viadana, should be used only for passages in full harmony, and here this is the most satisfactory method.

1 H. F. Redlich, *Claudio Monteverdi*, London (1952), p. 132.
  L. Schrade, *Monteverdi*, London (1951) (N.Y. 1950), p. 325.
  D. Arnold, *Monteverdi*, London (1963), pp. 150-3.

Editorial procedures

1.   Note-values have been left in the original in the outer sections in duple time, but quartered in the triple time middle section. The exact proportional relationship between the two original time-signatures, C and $O\,\frac{3}{1}$, remains doubtful; the suggested solution that two bars of the triple should equal one of the duple seems to work well in practice.

2.   All tempo, dynamic, ornament and *solo* and *tutti* markings are editorial.

3.   Regular modern barring, numbering and the double barring between the main sections are editorial. There are some bar-lines in the original where the rhythm becomes particularly *concitato* (e.g. from bar 206).

4.   All notes and accidentals printed small are editorial; accidentals redundant by the modern convention are omitted without comment. Some rhythm-signs have also been added in a few places to remind performers that the dotted figure in bar 1 should probably be applied consistently throughout.

5.   Ligatures in the original are noted by the usual square slur ⌐—¬, and coloration by brackets ⌐ ¬. Editorial slurs and ties have a short stroke through the middle ⌒╪.

6.   Spelling and punctuation have been modernised in accordance with present-day usage. All text added by the editor, whether indicated by ditto marks or simply omitted in the original, is printed in italics.

7.   The trombones follow the three lowest parts, except for sections marked *solo*. In a few cases simplifications of awkward passages have been suggested by printing stems attached to the notes (*e.g.* bar 16).

8.   The two violin parts have been interchanged, Violin I now being Violin II and vice versa.

Textual commentary

Bar 39, Tenor 2: crotchet rest missing.

,, 41, Tenor 2: orig. crotchet A plus crotchet rest.

,, 48, Alto: both Fs have a sharp before them, otherwise a mistake might be suspected. Perhaps the editorial sharp in the Continuo is unnecessary, however harsh the resultant false relation.

,, 57, Tenor 1, 2nd note: orig. has F for E (*cf.* Violin 2, bar 55).

,, 62: Original t-s $O\,\frac{3}{1}$, note-values quartered in edition. Alto has:

> Iucundus homo
> In memoria eterna   ⎱
> Paratum cor eius   Tacent
> Dispersit   ⎰

,, 80, Soprano 2: orig. dotted A, no rest.

,, 114, Continuo, 2nd note: orig. has D for F.

,, 133, Tenor 2: orig. 3 crotchets, no dot.

,, 151, Bass: orig. dotted A, no rest.

,, 201, Soprano 2 and Tenor 2: consecutive octaves *sic*.

Acknowledgments

My thanks are due to the Library of the Gesellschaft der Musikfreunde, Vienna, for providing a microfilm of the original part-books, and to the University of Sydney, which generously provided funds to aid my researches. I wish to record my gratitude to my former colleagues in the University of Sydney Music Department, Professor Donald Peart, Mr Simon Harris and Mr Eric Gross for their helpful and critical comments at various stages of this edition's completion, and to the members of the University Pro Musica Society, whose performances of the work provided a practical test for it. My thanks also to my present colleagues, Professor Peter Platt and Mr Laughton Harris who gave valuable assistance with the proof-reading.

Music Department   JOHN STEELE
University of Otago   1 September 1964
Dunedin, N.Z.

CLAUDIO MONTEVERDI

BEATUS VIR

(Psalm 111, Authorised Version 112)

for SSATTB chorus,
instruments and organ

edited from the
Selva Morale et Spirituale, Venice (1641) by

JOHN STEELE

NOVELLO PUBLISHING LIMITED

Order No: NOV 070212

BEATUS VIR

CLAUDIO MONTEVERDI
Edited by John Steele

*Or Viola I, Viola II, Violoncello. Instruments are optional; see Preface.

© *Novello & Company Limited 1965*

19347

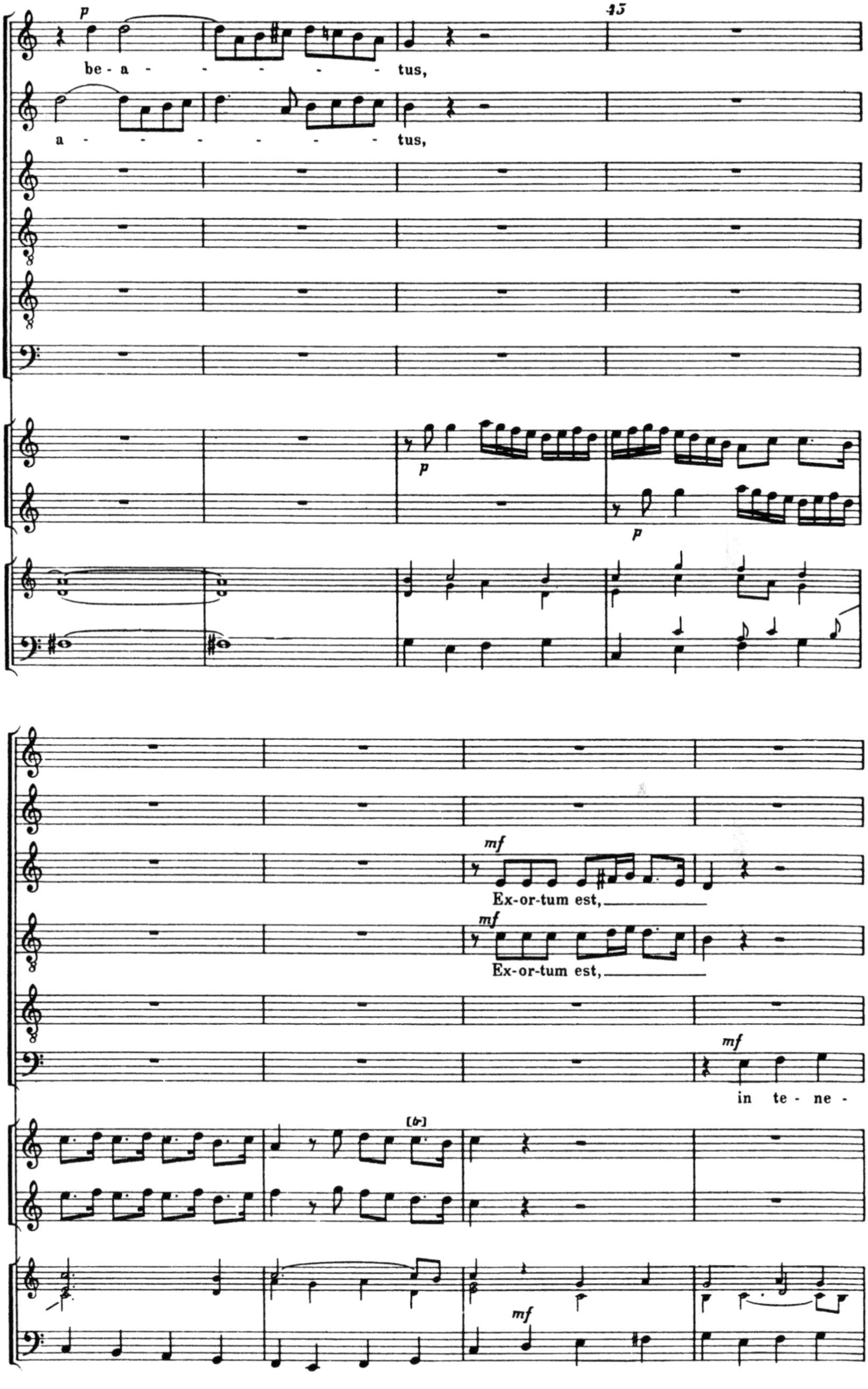
45
be-a- - - - - - tus,
a - - - - - - - tus,
Ex-or-tum est,
Ex-or-tum est,
in te-ne-

Printed and bound in Great Britain by
Caligraving Limited Thetford Norfolk